HIPPO

by Caroline Arnold
Photographs by Richard Hewett

MORROW JUNIOR BOOKS · NEW YORK

PHOTO CREDIT: Permission to use the following photographs is gratefully acknowledged: Arthur Arnold, pages 10–11 (top) and 16.

Library of Congress Cataloging-in-Publication Data. Arnold, Caroline. Hippo / by Caroline Arnold ; photographs by Richard Hewett.   p.   cm. Summary: Presents the characteristics and habits of hippopotamuses in the wild and of a family at the San Francisco Zoo.   1. Hippopotamus.] 1. Hewett, Richard, ill.   II. Title.
QL737.U57A76 1989   599.73'4—dc19   ISBN 0-688-08145-2 | ISBN 0-688-08146-0 (lib. bdg.)   88-39794   CIP   AC

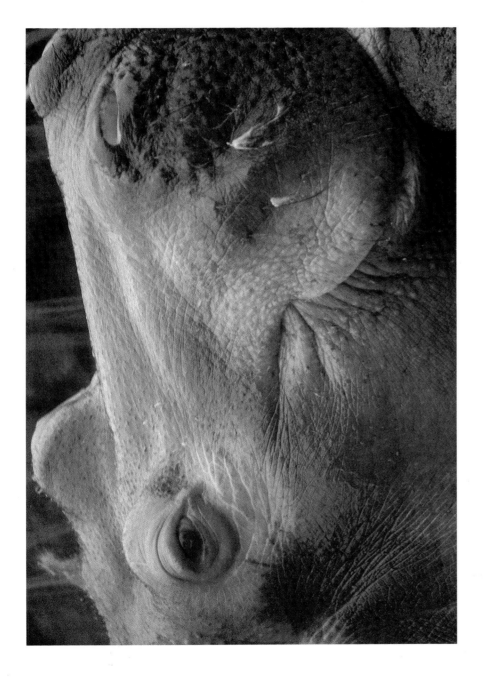

ACKNOWLEDGMENTS

We express our sincere appreciation to all the people at the San Francisco Zoo who helped us with this project. In particular, we thank Mike Sulak, Curator of Mammals; Ellen Newman, Director of Publicity; and all the hippo keepers. We also thank the Los Angeles Zoo; the California Academy of Sciences, Steinhart Aquarium; and Wildlife Safari, Winston, Oregon, for their assistance with the photographs. And, as always, we thank our editor, Andrea Curley, for her continued enthusiasm and support.

Pressed close to his mother's giant body, Doodles, a young hippopotamus, waited for the pool in their enclosure to fill with water. After a night spent inside, it would feel good to get wet again. From the time he was born six months earlier, Doodles had been able to swim and walk. Like all hippos, he was completely at home both in water and on dry land.

The young hippo and his parents live at the San Francisco Zoo in California. Like many of the animals there, the hippos had been named by the zoo staff. Perhaps because they are such strange-looking animals, they had all been given rather silly names. Doodles' mother was called Cuddles, and his father was named Puddles.

During the day, Doodles, Cuddles, and Puddles stayed in the front of their enclosure where zoo visitors could see them. Then, at night, they went into a large barn in the back.

The hippo exhibit at the zoo was made to be as natural as possible. In addition to the pool, it had an island, grassy banks, and a shady area for resting. The hippos seemed comfortable there and behaved much as they would in the wild.

When the pool was almost full, Doodles climbed up onto the island and walked to the edge. For a few minutes, he looked around, and then, with a giant splash, he dove in.

Like the hippos in their native home in Africa, Doodles and his parents spend most of every day in or near the water. As they eat, drink, play, and rest there, people stop to watch these remarkable mammals whose compact bodies look something like tiny gray-brown submarines. No other land animal except for the elephant is as large as the hippo, which, when fully grown, can weigh as much as 4 tons (3,628 kilograms)!

In the wild, hippos are found only in Africa south of the Sahara Desert. Sometimes called river hippos or Nile hippos, they live in rivers, in lakes, and occasionally even in ocean lagoons. Usually they gather in groups, some-times called *schools*, which vary in size from five to forty animals. In the water, a hippo herd often looks like a cluster of small islands, and, in fact, birds sometimes use these movable plat-forms as resting places.

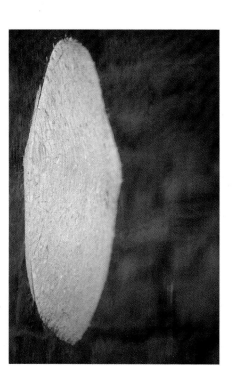

Hippo herd in the Nile River, Uganda.

Female hippos and their babies generally form a group that is separate from the males. This group, which is called the *crèche*, is closely guarded by the females. If a mother hippo must leave the crèche for a short time, one of the other female hippos acts as a baby-sitter for her youngster until she returns.

Males gather around the females at the edge of the crèche. Each male defends a small territory, which is called a *refuge*. The refuges closest to the female herd are usually occupied by the older, stronger males. A male may sometimes visit the female herd, but he must behave quietly. If he does not, the females quickly chase him out.

Young Nile hippo.

The scientific name for hippos is *Hippopotamus amphibius. Hippopotamus* comes from Greek words meaning "river horse." Although hippos do have long snouts like those of horses, the two animals are not closely related. *Amphibius* comes from Greek words meaning "both lives" and refers to the fact that hippos live both in water and on land.

During the Ice Age, which lasted from 40,000 to 10,000 years ago, a hippopotamus very similar to those that live in Africa today was common throughout most of Europe. A smaller variety lived in southern Europe, Asia, and North Africa. Today, all of these early hippos are extinct.

The only close living relation of the familiar *Hippopotamus amphibius* is the much smaller pygmy hippopotamus that lives in the rain forests of West Africa. Its scientific name is *Choeropsis liberiensis*. An adult pygmy hippo is about 5 feet (1.5 meters) long and stands only 2½ feet (.76 meter) high. It weighs about 600 pounds (272.7 kilograms). Although similar in shape to the larger hippo, it has a rounder head, larger nostrils, eyes that do not stick out, and smaller feet with sharp nails.

Unlike its larger relative, the pygmy hippo spends most of its life on land. It is active chiefly at night when it searches the forest floor for tender shoots, leaves, and fruits to eat. Pygmy hippos usually live alone or in pairs. They have always been rare, and although they are protected by law, their numbers are decreasing in the wild, and they are in danger of extinction.

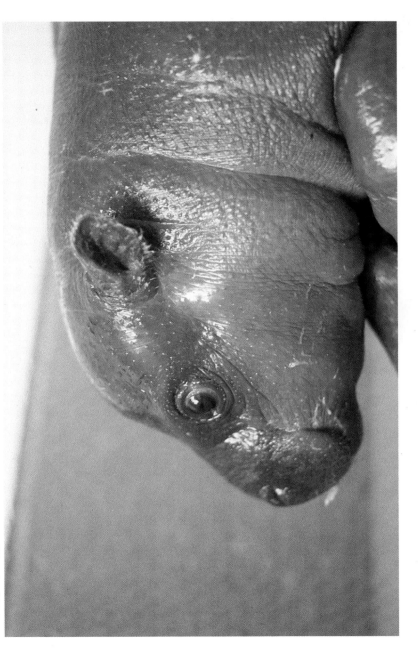

Baby pygmy hippo.

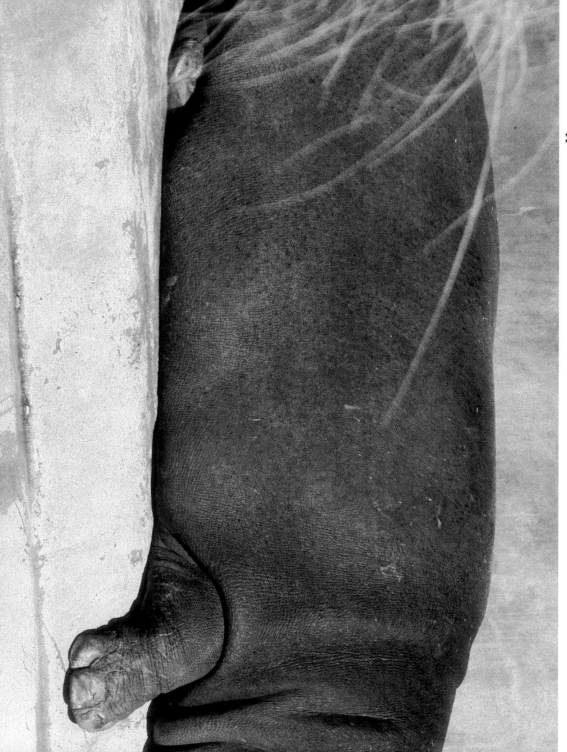

Female hippo.

The most outstanding features of the hippopotamus are its enormous size and barrel-shaped body. Short trunk-like legs support a stout body that sags to just a few inches from ground level when the hippo is upright. Underneath the saggy, gray-brown skin is a layer of fat several inches thick.

Large animals like hippos are extremely difficult to weigh. In cases when adult hippos have been accurately weighed, their sizes varied from 3,000 to 8,000 pounds (1364 to 3636 kilograms). An adult hippo stands about

5 feet (1.5 meters) tall at the shoulder and is about 14 feet (4.3 meters) long.

Male and female hippos look alike, although males are usually somewhat larger. Males also have larger *jowls*, or folds of skin that hang down on either side of the mouth. As with cattle, males are called *bulls* and females are called *cows*. Baby hippos are called *calves*.

In the wild, when one of the females is ready to mate, she selects a male from one of the nearby refuges. Mating takes place in the water, usually accompanied by a great deal of noise and splashing.

Male hippo.

The birth of a baby hippo takes place seven to eight months after mating. In Africa, most baby hippos are born during April and October. These are the months that follow the two rainy seasons. Then the grass is high and there is plenty to eat.

A hippo birth may take place either on land or underwater. If the baby is born in the water, the mother will push it up to the surface for its first breath of air. Usually, however, the female hippo leaves the herd shortly before her baby is due and finds a quiet, hidden place on shore to give birth. Although twins are sometimes born, female hippos usually have just a single baby.

A newborn hippo weighs between 40 and 60 pounds (18.1–27.2 kilograms). It is about 3 feet (91 centimeters) long and about 1½ feet (46 centimeters) tall. This is a giant compared to most other animal babies, but it is tiny next to an adult hippo. The baby is able to stand on wobbly feet within hours after its birth.

In the wild, the first weeks are the most dangerous time of a young hippo's life. Fully grown hippos are so large that they have no natural enemies except for people. However, young hippos must watch out for hungry crocodiles and lions lurking at the water's edge. The baby's mother stays close by her calf to protect it from these enemies.

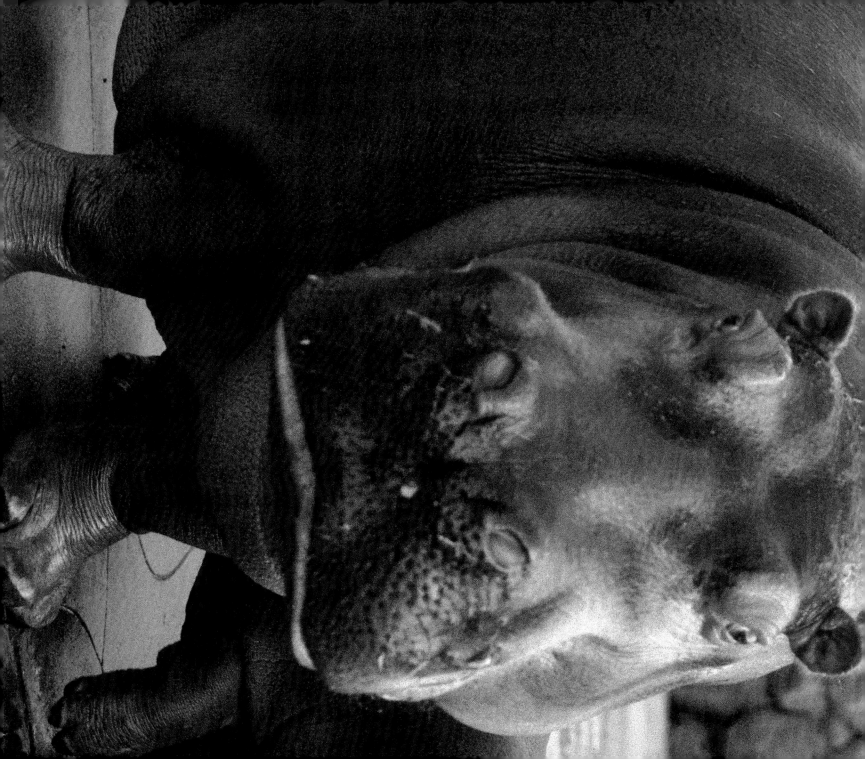

A hippo mother usually stays away from the herd for several weeks until her baby is strong enough to follow her easily. At the zoo, Doodles and Cuddles stayed by themselves until Doodles was about five weeks old.

From the time it is born, a hippo youngster must learn to obey its mother. On land, the young hippo is taught to walk level with the mother's head, where she can see it. If the mother quickens her pace or stops, her baby must do the same. If not, the mother punishes it by bumping it with her head. In the water, a mother hippo often lets her newborn baby ride or rest on her back. Then, as the baby becomes a stronger swimmer, it learns to swim by her side.

By the time Doodles and Cuddles rejoined Puddles in the larger enclosure, Doodles had nearly doubled his birth weight. As with all baby animals, he had a big appetite. His only food for the first few months was milk, which he drank from the teats on his mother's underside.

Because hippos spend so much of their lives in lakes and rivers, a baby often nurses underwater. Hippos can stay submerged for up to five minutes at a time. They can eat, walk, and even sleep underwater, coming to the surface every few minutes to get a breath of air.

Hippos are well adapted for their aquatic lives. Their eyes, ears, and nostrils stick up from the tops of their heads. This allows them to see, hear, and breathe while keeping the rest of their bodies hidden beneath the water.

When it is time for a breath, the hippo may lift up its whole head, snorting and shaking its ears to get rid of the water, or it may stick up only its nose. Each hippo nostril, which can open and close as needed, looks like a tiny volcano emerging from the wa-

ter's surface. Then, after breathing fresh air, the nostrils close, and the hippo submerges again.

Hippos rely on hiding in the water to escape from their human enemies. Although most wild hippos live in the safety of animal preserves and national parks, in places where they are not protected they are hunted for their tasty meat, strong hides, and valuable ivory tusks. By diving underwater, they can quickly disappear when it becomes necessary.

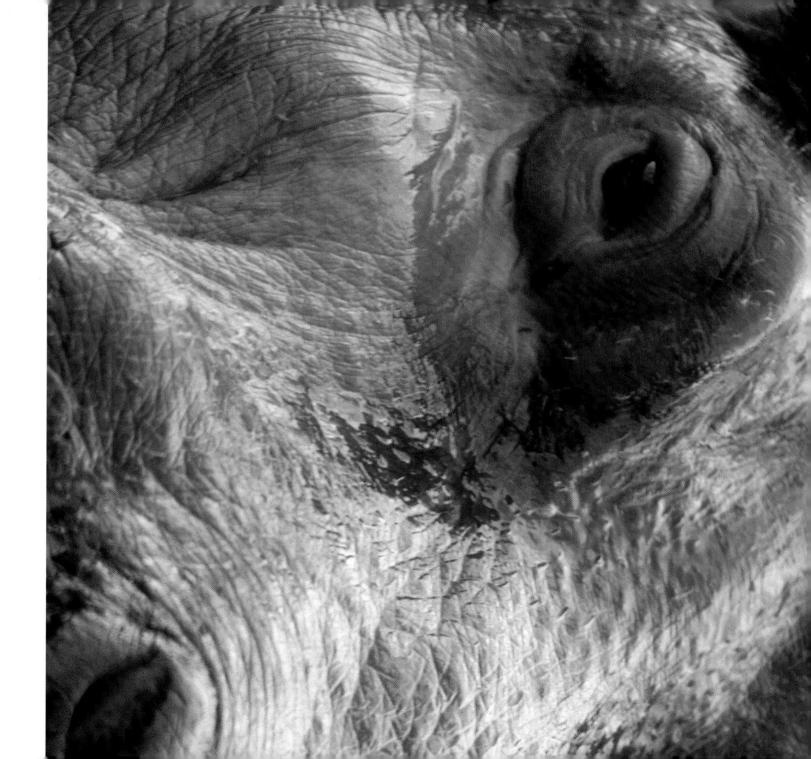

Another reason that hippos spend so much of their time in the water is to protect their tender skin. Unlike the skin of most mammals, which is covered with hair or fur, hippos have almost no hair. The little hair they have includes just a few bristles on the tail, ears, and snout.

In the hot sun, their skin can dry out and crack. Sometimes a red-colored liquid that looks like blood oozes out of the skin. Actually, it is a kind of sweat that helps keep the hippo's skin moist.

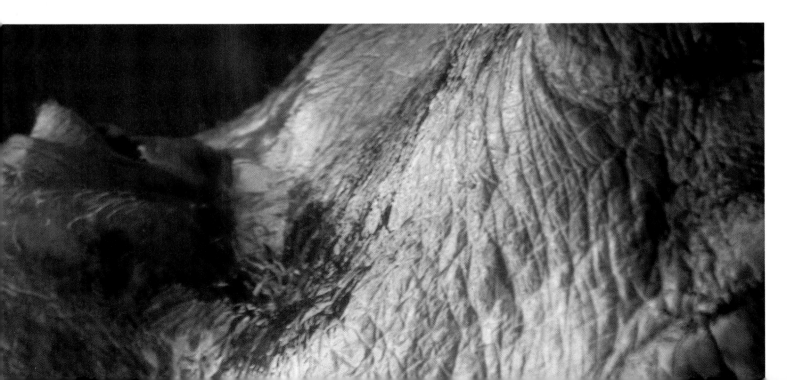

As Doodles became older, he grew rapidly. By the time he was six months old, he weighed about 500 pounds (227.3 kilograms). Although he still drank milk, he had begun to eat hay, like his parents. The hippos were fed twice a day, once in the morning and once in the late afternoon.

An adult hippo has an enormous appetite and eats up to 100 pounds (45.5 kilograms) of food each day. At the zoo, the animals' daily diet includes grain, alfalfa hay, sweet potatoes, carrots, cabbages, and a variety of other vegetables.

Unlike most animals, whose bodies float, a hippo is heavier than water. This allows the hippo to sink to the lake or river bottom, where it walks along looking for water plants to eat. Hippos can move at a rate of about 8 miles (12.9 kilometers) per hour underwater.

Hippos are vegetarians. In addition to water plants, they also eat grass, leaves, and other vegetable material on shore. On land, a hippo feeds by grasping its food in its lips and swinging its head from side to side to break off the plants. The hippo's giant, fleshy tongue moves the food to the back of the mouth, where it is chewed with flat molars before being swallowed. A hippo's stomach has three chambers, or compartments, through which the food moves and where it is digested slowly and thoroughly.

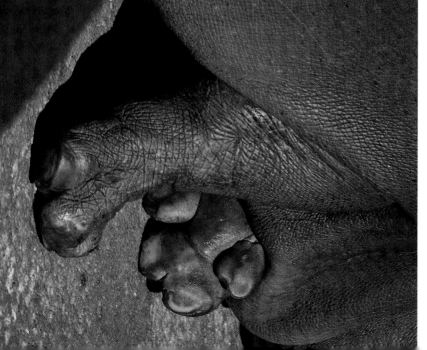

In the wild, hippos feed mostly at night, when they leave their ponds to graze on shore. Often, they must travel far to find enough food to satisfy their enormous appetites. Despite their ungainly appearance, hippos can run easily and can keep up a pace of 40 miles (64.4 kilometers) an hour over very long distances.

Hippos have four toes covered with hoof-like nails on the bottom of large, round feet. They belong to the large animal group called Artiodactyla, the even-toed hoofed animals. This group includes pigs, camels, deer, and many other animals. Hippos use their large feet to trample paths through the bushes surrounding their ponds to go to their nighttime feeding areas.

At dawn, the hippos return to the water, along the same trails they had followed earlier. They know how to find their way because they can smell their dung, which they have deposited near the beginning of the trail.

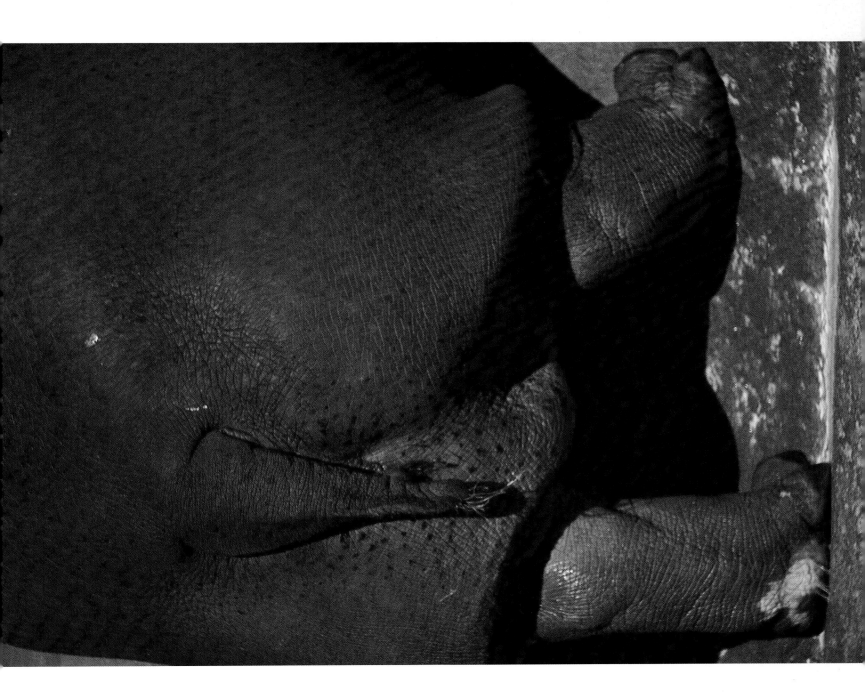

Occasionally, hippo herds grow so big in certain areas that there is not enough food nearby for all the animals. Then they may invade farmers' fields at night and destroy their crops. This is what happened in western Uganda in the 1960s. Wildlife managers had to reduce the size of the hippo herds to help restore the balance between the hippos and the natural food supply.

Hippos play an important role in nature in and near African waterways. The paths they make are often used by other animals that come to the water to drink. In the water, the hippos' dung provides nutrients for algae and water plants to grow. When the hippos walk along the river and lake bottoms they stir up sediment and plant matter, which provides food for fish. The fish in turn become food for birds and other animals that live at the water's edge.

Perhaps the most awesome feature of a hippo is its giant jaws. When the hippo opens them, it reveals the biggest mouth of any mammal except the whale. Inside the mouth are forty enormous teeth and four large tusks. The tusks grow to a length of 30 inches (76.9 centimeters) or more and the sharp incisors in the front of the mouth grow to an average of 20 inches (51.3 centimeters). Both the tusks and incisors grow continuously during a hippo's life.

A hippo's tusks and front teeth are extremely sharp. Because they meet at an angle, they act like giant scissors when the hippo closes its mouth. Hippos use their teeth for defense and to bite and slash one another when fighting. A female hippo will fight with any hippo that comes too close to her baby. Males fight with one another to get a chance to mate with a female.

Although a male hippo may be able to mate when he is five or six years old, he usually does not get a chance to do so until he is able to win a place close to the female herd. To challenge another animal to fight, the hippo emits a series of loud, honking snorts and then opens his mouth as wide as he can. Sometimes the weaker hippo will withdraw at this point. If not, the two animals then lunge at each other head to head, each trying to bite the other's front legs. In the wild, the skin of an older male is usually dented by scars earned in a lifetime of battles.

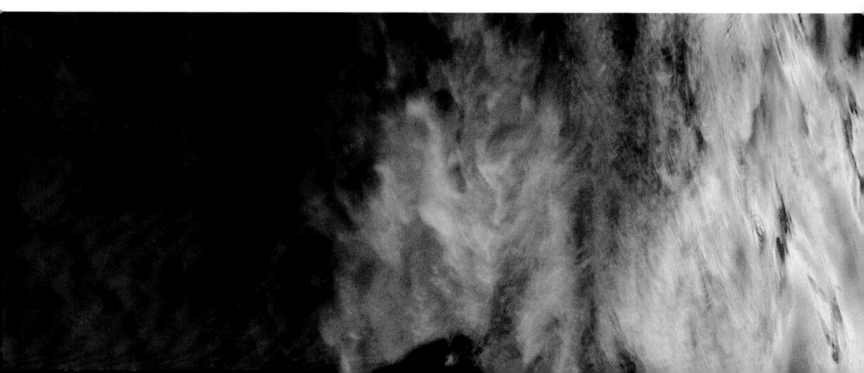

In the wild, young male hippos practice-fight with each other from a very early age. Doodles was already learning to practice-fight with his father. In these play battles, he would open his mouth and then grab hold of his father's lip. Puddles did not seem to mind Doodles' play attacks and always seemed careful not to hurt his son. When Puddles got tired, he just pushed Doodles away.

Like all young animals, Doodles was full of energy and liked to play. Young hippos in the wild usually play with other hippos of the same age in their herd. Their games include a kind of hide-and-seek and rolling in the water. Since Doodles had no other youngsters as playmates, he romped with his parents. In the pool, one of his favorite activities was doing somersaults over the big hippos' backs. They did not seem to mind when he climbed up on top and then rolled off to the other side.

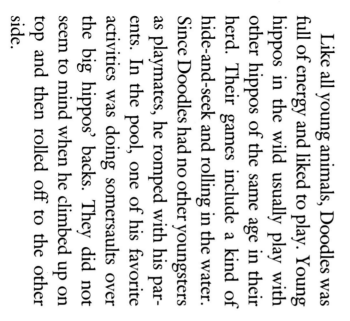

At the end of each day, Doodles and his parents got out of their pond to go into their nighttime enclosure. Only then was it safe for their keeper to enter the pool area to drain the water and clean the bottom. Although hippos do not normally attack people, they will do so if provoked. They are so big that any encounter is dangerous. People must be careful to stay a safe distance away from them.

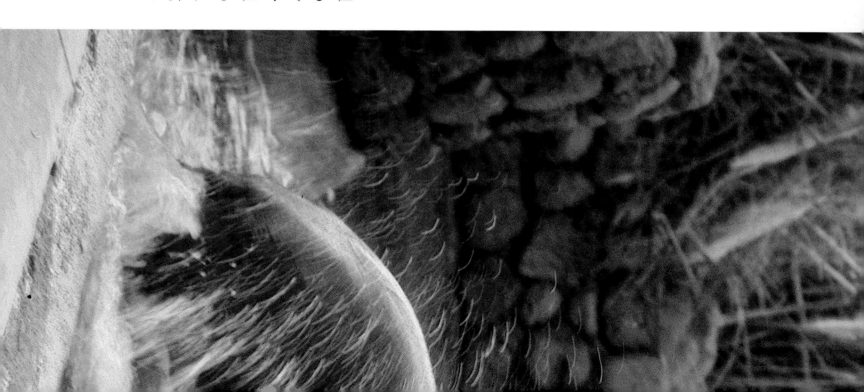

In Africa, young hippos stay with their mothers in the safety of the herd until they are about four years old. Sometimes a female hippo gives birth to a new baby when her first is two or three years old. Then she has two youngsters to look after until the older one can be on its own. When the family group leaves the water to feed on land, the young hippos follow their mother, youngest first and oldest last.

At four years of age, a young hippo is nearly the same size as its parents. At this age a young male goes off by himself and fights with other males for a territory of his own. Young females stay with the herd. A female hippo may be able to mate as early as three years of age, but often does not produce her first calf until she is seven or eight.

Doodles will stay with his parents at the zoo until he is about eight months old. Then he will go to a new home at another zoo. Even though he

will be only partly grown, he will no longer need his mother's milk and will be able to take care of himself.

Doodles has grown rapidly since he was born and soon he will be too heavy to transport easily. At eight months, he will weigh about 800 pounds (363.6 kilograms). By two years he can weigh as much as 2,000 pounds (909.1 kilograms). He will not reach his full adult weight until he is four years old or more.

In the wild, hippos usually live to be about thirty years old, and in captivity they have been known to live as long as forty-nine years. Cuddles and Puddles have been at the San Francisco Zoo for more than twenty-five years. Since 1970, they have produced a new baby hippo about once every eighteen months. Doodles is their twelfth offspring. After he leaves, they will probably mate again and produce a new baby.

People have been fascinated by hippos for a long time. Nearly two thousand years ago a hippo was placed on exhibit in ancient Rome. The first hippo to be exhibited in modern Europe came to the London Zoo in 1850. Today, you can see hippos in zoos all over the world.

Few of us will have the chance to observe hippos in their natural home in Africa. However, by watching them in zoos and wildlife parks we can find out more about them and learn to appreciate their unique adaptations to life in and near the water.

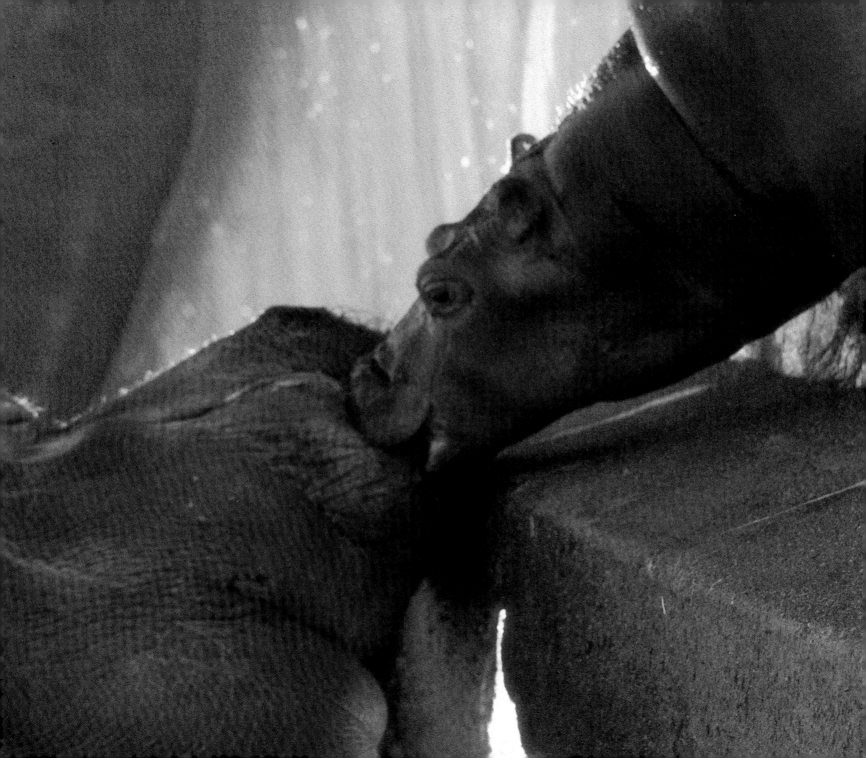

INDEX

Illustrations are in **boldface.**